THINK POSITIVE

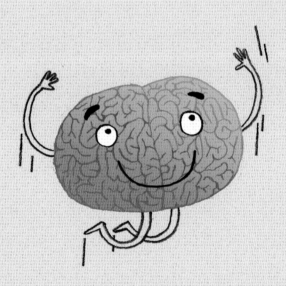

Written by Alice Harman
Illustrated by David Broadbent

W
FRANKLIN WATTS
LONDON·SYDNEY

Franklin Watts
First published in Great Britain in 2020 by The Watts Publishing Group
Copyright © The Watts Publishing Group, 2020

Produced for Franklin Watts by
White-Thomson Publishing Ltd
www.wtpub.co.uk

ISBN (HB): 978 1 4451 6925 5
ISBN (PB): 978 1 4451 6926 2
10 9 8 7 6 5 4 3 2 1

Alice Harman has asserted her right to be identified as the author of this
Work in accordance with the Copyright, Designs and Patents Act 1988.

Series Designer: David Broadbent
All Illustrations by: David Broadbent

Every attempt has been made to clear copyright. Should there be any
inadvertent omission please apply to the publisher for rectification.

Printed in China

Franklin Watts
An imprint of
Hachette Children's Group
Part of The Watts Publishing Group
Carmelite House
50 Victoria Embankment
London EC4Y 0DZ

An Hachette UK Company
www.hachette.co.uk
www.franklinwatts.co.uk

A trusted adult is a person
(over 18 years old) in a child's
life who makes them feel safe,
comfortable and supported.
It might be a parent, teacher,
family friend, care worker
or another adult.

MIX
Paper from
responsible sources
FSC® C104740
www.fsc.org

Facts, figures and dates were correct when going to press.

CONTENTS

A positive mindset

Do you think anybody can be **happy all the time** – never worried, never sad, never angry or scared or disappointed?

In a way that would be nice, **but it's just not realistic!** Humans naturally feel all sorts of emotions, and nobody on Earth has felt happy for every single second of their life.

What we can do, though, is train our brains to **focus on the good** rather than the bad in any situation – even when we're worried, or when things don't turn out as we planned.

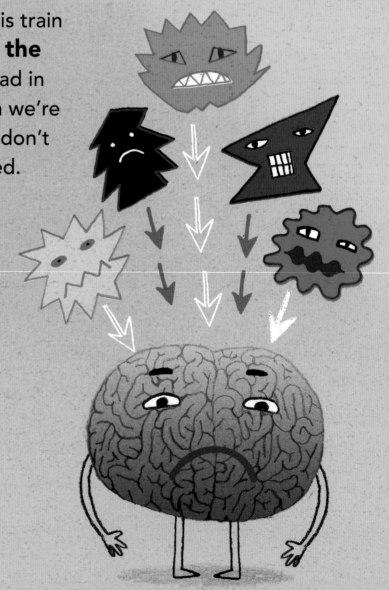

This helps our brains understand that things really can change for the better, and that we have the power to help make that happen.

We often think about our brains as if they are fixed – some people are smart or confident and others aren't. But that's just not true. Your brain is changing all the time, and you can do all sorts of things to **help it grow!**

You have billions of neurons in your brain, which build bridges between themselves to pass around information. The more you have certain thoughts, the stronger those bridges get.

Over time, **thinking positively** means your 'I can do it!' bridges get stronger than your 'I can't do anything' bridges, so it actually gets easier and easier.

Sounds good, right? Let's get started!

Half-full or half-empty

Imagine you've just gulped down half a glass of your drink. You could **think positive** – 'Great, the glass is still half-full!' or **negative** – 'Oh no, now the glass is half-empty!' But the situation is exactly the same!

When we focus on the negative – what we don't have or think we can't do, what has gone wrong or could go wrong – the world can seem like quite a scary, unfair place. It can make us feel down and hopeless, so we don't want to do anything.

But by training our brain to look for the positive, we remind it of all the good stuff – what we do have, what has gone right, how **things can get better** and what we can do about it.

1.

Think about a time when things didn't go quite how you wanted them to. For example, maybe you got into an argument with a friend about something.

3.

On the other side, write down all the **positive thoughts** and feelings you remember having – there might not be any!

2.

Draw a line down the middle of a sheet of paper, to split it into two. On one side, write down all the negative thoughts and feelings you remember having – for example, you might have felt sad and been worried that your friend would stop speaking to you.

4.

Now try to find a **positive thought** and action for each negative thing you've written down. For example, 'I'm worried my friend will stop speaking to me' could become 'I have a chance to show them how much I care about our friendship – I can write them a note to tell them that.'

All or nothing

It can be easy to think in an **'all or nothing'** way – that a situation is either good or bad, that you can either do something or you just can't.

But this isn't really a helpful or realistic way of thinking. It can make us feel like we might as well not try at all, that things are stuck the way they are and there's no point making any effort to change them.

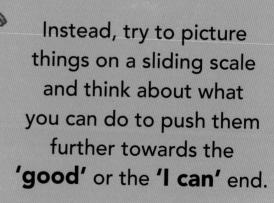

Instead, try to picture things on a sliding scale and think about what you can do to push them further towards the **'good'** or the **'I can'** end.

Maryam

When my school started a basketball club, I was so excited. At first, it all went really well. I really liked my teammates and I was the best at scoring baskets! Everyone started calling me the team's **'star player'.**

Then we played a game against another school's club. They were really good and I got so nervous that I didn't get in a single shot. We lost really badly, and even though everyone in my team was really nice I still felt terrible.

I told my mum I wasn't ever going back to the club because I'd let everyone down. But she reminded me that I was **part of a team,** and that my teammates weren't all thinking about me – they had their own performances to think about!

She also helped me see the positive side of the experience. I'd had a chance to see more advanced players in action and to learn how nerves could affect me, so I could set myself goals to keep improving.

I'm still going to the club now, and **I love it more than ever!**

Celebrate!

Our brains can be pretty impatient sometimes. As soon as we've finished something, or finally got the hang of something, they often want to **leap ahead** to the next thing right away.

But it's important to take a moment to **celebrate how hard you've worked!** It doesn't just make you feel good – it also makes it easier for your brain to remember it in future as a positive example of your hard work paying off.

Thinking back over times in the past when you've put in effort and succeeded helps your brain to believe that you can do it again! This can help you feel more **positive and confident** about facing new challenges.

Try making a **'Yes, I can!'** list that you can look at whenever you need a positivity boost.

On a sheet of paper, write down two or three examples of times when you found something challenging but worked really hard to finish it or get better at it.

It could be reading a tricky book, learning how to do a chore at home, talking to new people even though you feel shy – anything you like! Decorate each entry with some gold stars and coloured pencils so they all look really special.

Now create a second list – an **'I am learning to ...'** list – and write in things that you're working on at the moment. Every time you finish or make progress with something, tick it off this list and add it to your **'Yes, I can!'** list.

You could even say something nice to yourself each time, like 'Well done for putting in so much effort to finish that book, and not giving up when you got frustrated with how tough it was.'

Thanks for everything

We can often slip into focusing on **what we don't have**, rather than on all the brilliant things in our lives.

Taking a moment to list everything you're thankful for can make your brain **much happier.**

You may suddenly find that your worries about what you're missing out on **fade away** to nothing. Your brain has realised that your life is too full of other things to be thankful for.

Every day for a week, write or draw something that you're grateful for on a scrap of paper. Then **drop it in a jar.**

It could be anything you like – a tasty dinner, a friend who makes you laugh, a big hug from your mum or dad, your favourite cartoon, a **nice teacher**, your comfy bed!

At the end of the week, empty the jar and look through all the scraps of paper. You could even close your eyes and imagine yourself surrounded by all these wonderful things!

Keep adding to your jar, and read the scraps of paper whenever you need a reminder of everything you have to be **thankful for.**

Smile!

Sometimes, if you're feeling worried or upset, it can be really hard to think positively at all. To get in a more helpful mood, a smile or laugh can help give your brain a quick **positivity boost.**

When you **smile and laugh**, it releases chemicals in your brain – including ones called serotonin and endorphins – that help make you feel happier.

Laughing also helps to lower the level of cortisol in your brain – that's a chemical linked to feeling really worried.

But if you're feeling down, how are you supposed to break out into a grin or a giggle in the first place?

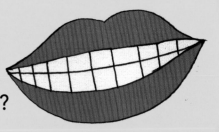

Here are some ideas to try out ...

1. Make a load of **funny, scrunched-up** faces, and imagine your face turning to jelly between each one! It's a fun way to relax the muscles in your face, which can get tense when you're worried or upset.

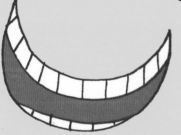

2. Think of something that's made you **laugh or smile** before – a cute animal video, a silly joke in a movie, or something funny that your friend said.

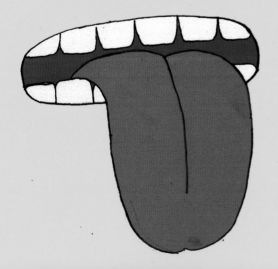

3. Watch and listen to other people laughing – whether it's in real life or on a video. Seeing and hearing **people laugh** can make our brain want us to do the same!

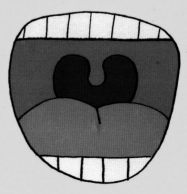

Truly positive

Thinking positive can be really helpful, but **it doesn't mean pretending** that everything is fine when it isn't.

Real positive thinking isn't about ignoring problems, it's about looking for ways to work through them and feel good about yourself and your life.

If something is making you upset or worried, it's always best to talk about it with an adult that you trust – like a parent or a teacher.

Remember, you don't have to handle everything on your own – and no one wants or expects you to try to do that. Sometimes the **bravest, most positive thing** you can do is to ask for **help**.

Nerys

Last year, I started finding English **harder and harder.** It seemed like all of my friends in class were keeping up fine with the tougher books and activities, and I was too embarrassed to say that I didn't really understand what we were doing.

I started **copying answers** off the people who sat either side of me in class. I worried about falling further and further behind over time, but I just tried not to think about that.

The teacher set us some homework to do with one of the books – a sort of diary to fill in over the next couple of weeks, with our own ideas – and I realised that I needed to **stop pretending** it was all OK.

I spoke to my teacher after class and **asked for help,** and he was really nice about it. Now I know I can always speak up if I get lost, and my dad is helping me with extra reading at home.

Let it go

In life, annoying little things just happen sometimes! Drinks get spilled, toys get broken, it rains when you want to go outside ...

Rather than letting these things spoil your day by making you angry and upset, try taking a deep breath and **letting them go.**

Then thank yourself for doing something really good for your brain!

It's happier and works better when you have a **positive attitude.**

Ricardo

What an annoying day! First, **a car splashed muddy water on my legs** as I walked to school. Then I realised my mum had given me my brother's lunchbox, so I had a sandwich I didn't really like. THEN my friend Laura accidentally broke my favourite pen, which I'd just lent to her for a second.

It could have turned into the worst day ever. I felt myself getting angry, and I remembered times in the past when I'd got really annoyed by little things like this.

I'd snapped at my friends and been rude to my teacher, and it had made everything ten times worse. It also **made me feel really bad** later on, when I'd calmed down.

Rather than getting into all that, I just took a deep breath, smiled and thought **'Let it go'.** It didn't magically stop me feeling annoyed, but it got easier every time I practised. And I felt really good that I'd made the decision to stay positive.

Feelings detective

Sometimes it's pretty easy to work out why you're **feeling negatively** about something – why you think you can't do it or don't even want to try it. For example, you might be scared to sign up for gymnastics club because you're worried you'll hurt or embarrass yourself.

But at other times you might just have the bad feeling and not quite know why. Then it's time to put on your detective hat and **try to work it out!**

Once you know what kinds of negative thoughts are going on behind the feeling, you can start working out how to deal with each one.

Think of something that makes you **feel worried** or upset, but you're not quite sure why. Write it down or draw it on a sheet of paper or a notebook page.

Underneath, write the question, **'What's the worst that could happen?'** Try to answer it, and write down or draw how you think that would make you feel.

It might not feel very nice to think about this, so do this activity with an adult you trust and talk with them about it.

What positive actions can you take so that you feel better about what might happen? Write or draw them, and make a plan with a trusted adult about putting them into practice.

Well done, Detective!

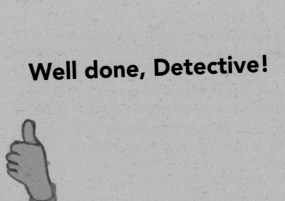

Seeing the future

For our brains, sometimes seeing is believing! Using a technique called **visualisation** can really help your brain think positively about the future.

Visualisation means **creating a picture** in your mind of something you would like to happen.

The idea is that because the ways your brain works to imagine things and actually take action are linked, visualisation helps your brain think of this positive result as more realistic.

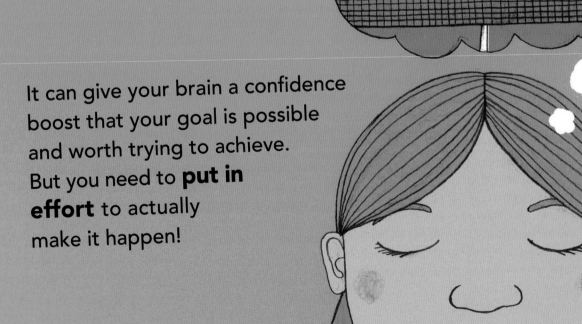

It can give your brain a confidence boost that your goal is possible and worth trying to achieve. But you need to **put in effort** to actually make it happen!

Draw a picture of something that you want to try to do better. For example, if you play a musical instrument and want to improve at it, you might draw a picture of yourself practising for 15 minutes every day.

Underneath this picture, write down three steps to help you achieve this. For example, to keep up your **musical practice** you could:

1. Decide on a set time that you're going to practise and ask an adult to help remind you.

2. Start a practice journal and keep a note of every day you practise.

3. Video yourself playing once a week, so that if you ever feel like skipping practice you can watch back and see how much it's helping you improve.

Positive people

Can you think of someone who always tries to see the **good in people** and look on the bright side of life?

People like this can make us **feel really good** about ourselves, too – as if we can do anything we put our mind to, and that even if we don't get it right away it's all going to be okay.

There are others who tend to see things in a **negative way** – complaining a lot, thinking everything will turn out badly and maybe even putting you down. This can really drain your positive energy.

If someone is being very negative and making you feel bad, try talking to them about it – they might not even realise they're doing it!

Sasha

Today was the **worst day ever.** Everything we had to do in class was really boring, and the activities were stupid.

Jonah, who sits next to me, was being so annoying. He knows we're both rubbish at science, but he nagged me until I looked at one activity. I couldn't do it, **so I gave up.**

Jonah

Today was great! Our teacher gave us activities all about wind power and how it can help the planet.

I have to try quite hard to understand things in science, so I find it really helpful when we have hands-on activities. I felt like I was really growing my brain today!

I tried hard **not to let Sasha's comments get me down,** and encouraged her to have a go – and she did! I felt proud of myself for handling that well.

DOING GOOD

Think back to the last time that someone was **really kind to you**. Maybe they helped you out, said something nice or listened when you were upset. How does thinking about it make you feel?

When people are kind to us, it can make us think **more positively** about ourselves and the world. That makes sense, right? But here's the interesting part – scientific studies have found that acting kindly towards others makes us happier, too.

When we know that we are doing something good and making life better for others, we feel proud of our behaviour. This gives our brains a positivity boost – and also makes us more likely to behave kindly in the future. **Everybody wins!**

Want to do something good for others, but not sure where to start? **Here are some ideas ...**

★ **Keep an eye out** at school for kids who look lonely or unhappy – sometimes a friendly chat can make someone's day

★ Offer to **help your parents** with tasks that need doing around the house

★ **Raise money** for a charity – it could be a cake sale, a sponsored swim, anything you like!

Ask your parents to help you care for the animals in your area – you could plant flowers that bees like to eat from, make a 'bug hotel' for minibeasts or put out food for birds to eat.

Be kind to yourself

Sometimes we can be really kind towards other people but really mean to ourselves!

Imagine if you had a friend who kept saying nasty, untrue things to you all the time – that you can't do anything, that you're not good enough, that people don't like you. You wouldn't want to keep them as a friend, would you?

But most of us know what it feels like to hear that nasty voice inside our own head, and we seem to put up with it more when it comes from ourselves.

It's really hard to be happy and try our best when we have these negative thoughts bouncing around inside our brains. So it's important to think about how to be a better, kinder friend to yourself.

The next time you have nasty, negative thoughts about yourself and all the things you think you can't do or don't deserve, write them down on a piece of paper.

But at the top of the page, write the name of someone you really like and care about. Imagine you're saying all of these horrible things to them – you never would, would you? How do you think it would make them feel if you did?

The fact that you're saying these things to yourself doesn't mean they hurt any less than if you said them to someone else. So on the other side of the page, write yourself a letter saying sorry for thinking all those mean things.

 In your letter, write some positive things to yourself instead – think about what you try hard to do, and tell yourself how proud you are for making those efforts.

Keep THINKING POSITIVE!

Read through these **positive-thinking** tips any time you need a quick reminder!

List your negative thoughts and try to find a **positive thought** or action for each one.

Rather than seeing situations as **all good or all bad**, picture a sliding scale and think what you can do to push things further towards the 'good' end.

When you make progress, take a moment to **celebrate** how hard you've worked!

Regularly write things down you're thankful for, and look back over them.

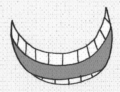 Find ways to make yourself **smile and laugh**, to release happy chemicals in your brain.

Tell a trusted adult if something is really worrying you – **thinking positive** doesn't mean pretending everything is fine when it isn't!

Don't let annoying little things spoil your day – take a deep breath and move on!

If you're not sure why you **feel negative**, talk with a trusted adult about what you're afraid might happen.

Visualise yourself making **positive changes**, and take steps to make this a reality.

If other people's constant negativity makes you feel bad, talk to them about it.

 Do kind and helpful things for each other – whether that's friends, family, animals or the planet.

Don't be mean to yourself! Talk to yourself kindly, like you would to a friend.

Notes for parents and teachers

The concept of a **'growth mindset'** was developed by psychologist Carol Dweck, and is used to describe a way in which effective learners view themselves as being on a constant journey to develop their intelligence. This is supported by studies showing how our brains continue to develop through our lives, rather than intelligence and ability being static.

Responding with a growth mindset means being eager to learn more, and seeing that making mistakes and getting feedback about how to improve are important parts of that journey.

A growth mindset is at one end of a continuum, and learners move between this and a 'fixed mindset' – which is based on the belief that you're either smart or you're not.

A fixed mindset is unhelpful because it can make learners feel they need to 'prove' rather than develop their intelligence. They may avoid challenges, not wanting to risk failing at anything, and this reluctance to make mistakes – and learn from them – can negatively affect the learning process.

Help children develop a growth mindset by:

- Giving specific positive feedback on their learning efforts, such as 'Well done, you've been practising …' rather than non-specific praise such as 'Good effort' or comments such as 'Clever girl/boy!' that can encourage fixed-mindset thinking.

- Sharing times when you have had to persevere learning something new, and what helped you succeed.

- Encouraging them to keep a learning journal, where they can explore what they learn from new challenges and experiences.

- Trying to use positive, action-focused language with them, while still making it clear that you don't expect them to be happy all the time – the aim is to avoid feeling stuck in bad feelings rather than not expressing them at all.

Glossary

attitude a way of thinking or feeling about something, which often affects how you act

neuron a type of cell, of which there are billions in your brain, that pass information back and forth between each other

visualisation picturing something in your mind that you would like to come true in future

Index